Just like how to a seed that lays unborn within the cold womb of earth, many storms reveal the strength and purpose of its birth. May the seasons of pain and change always reveal to you the Epiphany of love and life in full bloom.

To my family, to my readers–
Thank you for believing in me and pushing me to take the
leap even when I wouldn't believe. I hope these words give
you strength to move forward with gentle strides.

Athira Kamal

Happiness Is
a Butterfly

AUSTIN MACAULEY PUBLISHERS™

LONDON • CAMBRIDGE • NEW YORK • SHARJAH

ISBN – 9789948796381 – (Paperback)
ISBN – 9789948796398 – (E-Book)

Application Number: MC-10-01-1607898
Age Classification: E

Printer Name: iPrint Global Ltd
Printer Address: Witchford, England

First Published 2023
AUSTIN MACAULEY PUBLISHERS FZE
Sharjah Publishing City
P.O Box [519201]
Sharjah, UAE
www.austinmacauley.ae
+971 655 95 202

I would like to acknowledge an immensely heartfelt debt to Austin Macauley Publishers for their tremendous support at each step without which this book wouldn't have been brought before the readers. Special mention to the production team at Austin Macauley publications for their admirable guidance and support in the completion of the book.

I would also like to ardently thank my family for their constant care and love without which this book would never have been completed. Thank you for your unconditional love and trust in me.

Finally, loving thanks to Dubai for being my eternal inspiration and being home to my dreams.

Table of Contents

Section 1: Shadow

Before clarity there is confusion, before hope there is pain and before light that evades all darkness there is shadow.

Poem 1:
Midnight

The cold comes heavy tonight
Howls of anguished wolves
Not close yet not far away sound
Then closer I hear their prowl.
The tender dreams give away
as I lay dreamlessly
awake in pain.
Rather escape this dread
than fear
will dawn ever come again.
But I see light
tender and frail
seeping through
my broken window pane.
I clutch my empty soul
and rise again
yet again,
to face the precious dawn once more.
So give strength to my weary bones
As I dress with faint fingers
My hope, my dreams, and myself
of the floor.

Of pale gold pink sunlight soft
streaming through,
'Touch and give me love to go on.'

Poem 2:
Dreamless

Desolate midnight reveries
stumble upon my pastures of sleep
taking away only in patches and snatches
my pain and agony.
I star-gaze endlessly
gazing rather desolately
at the galaxies being projected
upon ceilings, walls in pieces
casting glimpses of
darkened walls and hangings.
As light shimmers to see them dangling
upon cold walls of plastered cements
for rather too long and too lonely.
But I hear you stirring
mumbling something in dreams,
catching you up in far off clouds and dwellings.
I hear you breathe, sighing
slowly bringing music to my tired eyes.

Poem 3:
Numb

How often have I succumbed to thee
my painful revelries
taking me to places I intend not to be,
in spite of all my troubles.

But being sedated on pain
keeps you floating
hoping sleep comes, in vain

to soften the tears that tumble
slowing them in shallow puddles
as sleep comes as sweet winter
dropping upon these lids

heavier than coal,
stooping them in soft motion falling now
lighter than snow.

I awaken and tremble
now in full awareness
of bones and muscles
that I never knew or cared to know

But the lashes are too tired to open
too bright the light
too loud the commotion.

Of self-questioning
full of doubts
but no answers

from the frail voice
deep inside asking,
"What happened?

to that little girl that believed and empowered,
dreams and strong powers
of the soul and hour
that heals all and leaves none
untouched by her caress.

So comfort now for relief will be here soon,
much soon
so believe."

Poem 4:
Trouble

Trouble is like an unrelenting child
that bothers one with screams and cries
at the top of its lungs
until you are deafened out
of your thoughts and all that's noble
in life here and beyond.
Silly they are but children ,after all
handle them with love
they will turn out just fine
so goes with trouble that comes unwelcomed into life.

Poem 5:
The Fight

The wolves have rounded up again
above these valleys and violet hills,
in my mind I tremble again
another day the same thing ,again.

Violet skies plump up the moon
hiding her behind the blue hue.

'Sit up straight, don't fall
Oh please, don't fall
Don't slack off
Don't drowse.'

Like poppies in the storm
my soul does sway

As I edge on the chaos of pain
and battle looking out
these windows in rain
To see if the sun will ever rise again

Amidst these howls
and their ghost white echoes
I wonder if the sun will rise again.

Poem 6:
Tunnel

I remember being here before
not much long ago
at first I had stumbled
over the debris and overgrown moss
I don't have much time I know

I must find a way out before it gets too dark
and uncomfortable
but my weary limbs tire out and wobble
asking me to stop
to not try much further

But I believe the tunnel must have an end
for every beginning there should be one they said
but days pass on to months
and months pass onto years

I feel I haven't budged even a little
Perhaps I have struggled
in leaving landmarks
in rubbles.

For in this place
everything looks grey and troubled
by weight of things
they hold unpowered.

I know I must find a way out
before the darkness doubles
or I will be lost here forever
in stubble.

No, I must struggle
no matter how long it takes me.

Poem 7:
The Forest

Remember when as a child
I wandered through forests
of dreams and sighs
pushing away branches
laden rich with colors
of every flower and fig
that grew through
the wet moss and fog
of uncertainties and still
pushing me through
to every goal and thrill.

But now the forest has grown
too thick and heavy

with leaves and fruits
dead and dizzy

for they breathe no more
of love or amore;

but pain of those realities
that one has to embrace with thorns
with strength and perseverance
to make out of this jungle
or to just end.

But what are those heady scents?
Of roses not,
the ones that drink and drench
the summer air;
but of lilies sweet and bright
standing tall
in the marsh of mind and chaos
Standing proud with purity and strength
as she lights my dark path
as I stumble and try
again.

Poem 8:
Pearls

Tears opulent roll down
in the vanity of the moonlight;
pale, purple, green, and blue
shimmering like pearls
caught against the dim light of the room.

"We have been here before," I hear
a strange voice of concern
muttering low
my inner wavering strength,
so fragile.
Questioning my intentions
doubting by my side,
over how I was to get on again
for so unbearable seems the pain.

"Weeping over things that won't change
merciless as the storm in rage
hush now, try to be brave:
be still
No matter how ever worn-out
you are from within

you have to rise up
for yourself again;
We have been here
before as always it has been
all I can say
for the puddles of tears
that pool beneath your feet—
beneath your dignity
only drowns your soul
and soak up the courage you need.

So get back up now
get back on your feet
for those watching you
behind these sullen doors
sadly holding on
hoping that you will heal
only break and shatter thinking about you
and the savage beast that eats you away.
For them let us be strong again
to give them courage let us be strong again."

I stir rather hopelessly
and in pain.
"Cheer up now," feebly she smiles,
"for you have people that love you
don't let them drown
in these merciless tears with you–

Be strong for them, for they wait
and hope the sunrise
will lift your foggy brows of pain.

For them let's be happy again."

I tumble as I get back on my feet
and close my tired lids
falling faster in peace
for tired heads and tired hearts
we have for now.

I need to rest to get back
to try and do the things I love
no matter how and forever it seems for now.

I daze through sleep that falls upon me like snow
waking up to watch the horizon low
rising above the foggy clouds of yesterday
are hopeful beams calling me to try again.

Poem 9:
The Ride

It's those silvery nights again
as we drive side by side
down this lonely path of life.

The long journey wears us down
and we silently feel the pang of love
that we left back home to return without;

And now we are left to fight on our own.
You dread of things that worry and bother you
of things that bully and those that taunt you.

I sit back and try to stop the ceaseless tears
as I silently wipe back the pain
I fear.

There comes another wave now
and then it's quiet for a while.
I struggle silently as I try to sleep again.

But I feel you reach out to me—
hold my hand so tenderly
for more than a sister you mean to me.

"I will always be by your side,"
says she as she slips to sit beside me
and hold me ever so lovingly.

In this space I may seem distant from you
for your words seem to echo through
walls I have built around my soul
lest I be left again
all alone.
But
I know you weep for me
Thank you for being there for me.

Even when you can't bear to see
Thank you for always being there for me.

Even though I can't say it now
Thank you for always being there for me.

Section 2: Light

However, dark the nights may be, however strong the storms may seem, daylight is bound to come in shards like a song. So always try to hold on. For only the brave weather the storm, only the courageous win battles so long—for only power can pull you through this war.

Poem 10:
Light

Shards of gold break through every corner
as the pale moon retreats sober
open up those tired eyes
there seems to be another light.
Another day that has come
to show what you have become
through the tempestuous dark atmospheres
you have sailed strangely to safety again.
Place those cold feet upon the ground
and feel the warmth seep the mount.
The weary nooks and corners dark
like willows twisted in the storm
of the body behind the pain
Wake up once again.

Poem 11:
Wildflowers

Salty rivers pooled down
the chasm of chaos and halted
as the dry earth
quivered its chapped lips open
to drink from the mercy
that grief brings unsought.
It was only yesterday,
that these rivers had frozen
but now as they flow down
again, once again
the summer air fills with smell of sweet wildflowers
that were born
along these empty lanes,
nourished and embraced
loved and watered
by these very waters
growing headlong along the salt and pain
learning to be strong once more.

Poem 12:
Wings

Are these wings that flutter behind me?
Feather soft ,like a cloud, airy
Melting with sunrise golden and lovely
I wonder;
How did those tears of yester and oceans of echoes
finally recede?
How did I make it yonder
when all the while I was drowning.
But here I am once more
another day
to watch the sunrise again.

Poem 13:
Words

The fire of words burn in me—
as I wince and wither to write them down,
the pen feels heavy against the soreness of my palm
But these words need to slip out somehow.
The wind waits with abated breath
upon the bleak emptiness of these white sheets,
as I stretch my mind and unwind from vicinity;
to try and reach the dark twisted corners in me
that try to speak and fail miserably
to utter anything other than stutters
like an engine empty with soot.
But this pen, these words are solace, comfort to me
for I know I have a friend in thee.

Poem 14:
Shore

It's time to fold up those tired wings
and settle upon these shores of peace.
Rest these weary feet still now
on the cool sands of yonder love.

Start again afresh tomorrow
for always
always there is hope in morrow.
Each unlike yesterday
each a new, each a prayer
of hope sent upwards in smoke
to Gods hidden behind the smog
of clouds and wondrous glow.

So start again—here again we go
The sun always shines the brightest
Through clouds of storms.

With you by my side
I will start again
and weave gardens of harmony again—
where little blue dews

drench green and all hues.

Not to soak wet like tears
that you and I have drunk so clear
But to watch as the pale gold of the warm sun rises anew
as I watch the sun rising in you.

Poem 15:
Escapism

How often have I ran away from here
to escape things that take me near
nearer and nearer to things
that I dread and fear.

Then in the ocean of pain
of anguish and helplessness
I close my eyes and float away
away on a sea of clouds.

As the sun rises above the crowd
of painful thoughts
I walk amongst lavender
and dill,
in happiness that finally ,an escape
only an escape can bring.

Releasing my soul from treacherous grips
that only cracks and shatters hope.
But here I am
at least for now
there is a wave of peace

floating

frothing by at my feet
as I dip and waddle here in ease

for now troubles seem to cease
numbing my senses to rest here
till I can gather and heave
to pull the heavy burden
of a heart
that has withered undue
to start again
to try again
to fill them with blooms anew.

Section 3: Home

To the city of dreams and miracles, to the place I call home. For being my sole comfort and companion as I ventured far away into lands uncertain.

Poem 16:
To Be Free

Free on the wings of poesy
flying higher and higher
I reach the strange mysteries unveiled to man,
the overturned cup of Heaven.
Up on the clouds I float
stepping on each delicate fluff of gold
bursting through as the sun is setting
over Isles of purple and gold.
The endless blue like an ocean behold
calling to me
to stay, never back to misery.
Oh! How light it feels to be carried off by
such beauty to only drink away.
The amber honey-colored trees
way down below, beckon to me.
But now I live under another sky
for me heaven now lies in the desert sighs,
the city's buzz and the summer skies.
So let's stay here under the canopy of love
and embrace the moment before it goes.

Poem 17:
Memories

It happened too long ago
now to remember
the uprooted cacti
that were once plush
with cool waters
of long gone summers and rain,
that once fell on my childish face.
Drizzling welcoming change
on cooler summer nights.
The pain comes not from reminiscences
but from wounds that still need healing.

But here the sands still remain golden,
the sunsets amber and the winds laden
with fragrances that bring me back to my oasis
as I find my childhood mirages come to life again.

Poem 18:
New Beginnings

Sometimes we cease becoming furious
Over things that haven't ended, yet
We stretch the darkness and shadows
Over the light that bravely enters
Of showers dripping down branches
That once though barren
Now lowers flowery branches
To embrace you and your new beginnings
For now, the storm has ended
And for now there will be light.

Poem 19:
Dreamers

Extravagant dreams
to sit still upon the dew-wet hill green
under a silver moon glistening,
whispers of the wind and sleepy wildflowers
to catch your breath in awe
To dance under the setting summer skies
pink fading to blue mauve
To stay there
To dream up dreams
Thoughtless
To be here
right now, without being swept away
by your past follies
And your future drudgeries.

Poem 20:
Winter in the City

The sun lowers its warm embrace
as the pink hued winter sky
lifts up her cloudy gaze
pinning back her little curls
revealing the pearly end
of a tiny moon
silently listening
to the evening prayers—
a call out to the faithful
and said
to wait on and believe in them
for the moon touches our desert's brows tonight
with powerful potions
of tender dreams unsaid.

Poem 21:
Old Souk

Walking by hand in hand
with the old and brand-new
through the golden city ways
husky with scents of brand hue;
spice sharp, salty, and oud.

Strolling by waters old
hovering in my streams of thought
as life bustles on
with a fire and passion,

that have passed these very waters prior
of fathers and forefathers,
dreamers and lovers
of those that adored these very lands
swaying upon these flowing waters

these waters that shine and sparkle
for time and time again
for time and times to come

of the land that gives hope
of this land I call home.

Poem 22:
Love

Life they say is impossible
without staggers and puzzles
that which make you question
all that matters and that which doesn't.

Pain is irreplaceable
for she is the foremost of teachers in life's lessons
pain is irreplaceable
but it must be erasable.

I believed you and thus persevered
in every pursuit to move and severe
penalties that pursued
me in every tussle.

I would have believed you wronged me
in telling lies so grievously ill
of things that would never cease and
never begin again;

until you healed me
and gave hope to my grieving soul

enabling me to be me
despite of struggles that may come unforeseen.
You give wings to dreams
the gold of cities
that believe in us
as we believe in thee.

Poem 23:
Boundless

Waking up to summer skies
of a city that bloomed so fine
with hopes and dreams alluring
golden like a diamond shining
upon the head of a goddess dancing.

You are the land of dreamers, seers, and prophets
that graced the earth with their presence and footprints
left behind to be followed
and not forgotten

paving paths for endless pursuits
to create fantasy out of thought
and shatter
the old abstractions
for nuances and rookies:

for craftsmen have engraved you
to become the beauty
they bestow you—
Elegance for art lovers
Home for the soul seekers.

Poem 24:
In a Trance

She twirled
tresses afloat in motion

arms above as in a trance begotten
reaching out towards the mauve, star-lit night sky

swaying to some unheard rhythm
beckoning to her in some strange unearthly wonder.

Dancing away blissfully to the mystic chants
only she could fathom and summon

about dreams conceived
under the canopy of million speckles

of the probable and the improbable
reaching to the moon and floating amongst the clouds

So rise in me and surge like the wind
so I too can sway with the hills of this desert.